C000128607

'Melancholic Moments:
A Poetry Chapbook'
Copyright © Tadhg Culley 2021.
Cover Image by Dids from Pexels

Contact the author at:
undotheheartbreak@gmail.com

ISBN: 9798548792037

Dedication:

I dedicate this to everyone who has traversed the mire of melancholia.

*"**Melancholia** or **melancholy** (from Greek: μέλαινα χολή melaina chole, meaning black bile) is a concept found throughout ancient, medieval and premodern medicine in Europe that describes a condition characterized by markedly depressed mood, bodily complaints, and sometimes hallucinations and delusions. "*

*"**Melancholic** [mɛlənˈkɒlɪk]*
ADJECTIVE
-feeling or expressing pensive sadness.
"their work often has a wistful or melancholic mood"
-suffering from or denoting a severe form of depression.
"patients with melancholic depression"

'Ripples'

The tide of my life is fast ebbing low,
The current's power? A much lesser flow...
The course is a trickle; such shallow streams.
Her Name, only whispered, vanquished my dreams.
The waves are withdrawing back to their source,
The riptide roars with diminished force,
The rippling water is soon running out;
Where heart and soul no longer sing nor shout,
When water returns to where it came from;

My words will remain but I shall be gone.

'Some'

Some carry lanterns to shepherd your way,
Some carry spotlights to show all your shame,
Some carry balm to heal your deep wounds,
Some carry knives to stamp out High Noon.
Some carry hugs to lessen your grief,
Some carry jokes to shun your relief,
Some carry peace to let you feel heard,
Some carry hate to spurn you from herd.
Some carry light to coat you in love,
Some carry night to bury your dove.

'Side-sea'

I went walking on a beach,
Beneath skin those waves did reach,
High walls of my heart were breached,
Down my cheeks, salt tears did teach:

"Moments go, they always do.
Nothing ever gets renewed.
Time is borrowed, hours are few.
Company is fleeting too..."

Hand-in-hand, walked with no-one,
Yet felt Presence; while alone...

'Dog and Man'

The young man and his dog,
Were perfect companions,
With food and water in bowl,
And squeaky donuts galore.

The young man and his dog,
Went on strolls around the town,
Breathing fresh air, hearing birds,
Sat on a bench, in the park.

The young man and his dog,
Loved each other completely,
Loyalty, both, through and through,
Wagging tails; spreading smiles.

The old man and his dog,
Easing down, a pace too slow,
Beating hearts, fading, tiring,
Glad to share life together.

The old man and his dog,
Savouring the scents they smell,
Favouring the routes they took,
Viewing blurry memories.

The old man and his dog,
Share one last treat to snack on.
Stroke one last touch; coat of fur.
Sleep one last time; dog on lap.

'Written Words Heard'

As I write these words,
And as you read them,
We share a moment,
Together; apart...

Strangers to each other,
Your eyes on my rhymes,
A message combines,
In one thought; alone.

My emotions spent,
On ink and paper,
Traverse lifetimes,
Where we will *both* die!

Yet here, you and I,
(In one magic moment),
Converse between Time,
In cosmic dance halls...

Spinning, vibrating,
Breathing, elating,
Sitting while thinking;
Ne'er leaving this book...

'In Those Dunes'

The sand between our toes,
Grass blades crushed into juice,
Sunrays shared in Heaven,
Coating skin golden brown.

Not doing anything,
Bellies full, *all* thirsts quenched,
Spring/Summer intertwined,
Mortality can wait...

Our work schedules *can wait,*
Our hopes, our dreams, *can wait.*
In this special moment:
Feeling so alive **HURTS**.

(Mortality ne'er waits).

'Dine On Each Day'

I could *eat* yesterday again!
My order was a beach road trip,
To favourite place; Prestatyn.
I walked my dog along the Sea.

We chased raindrops that rocked the tide,
Footprints and pawprints were aligned,
Feeling so free, so very alive,
I ate mussels, crab and cockles.

And then *melancholy* struck me!
Hearing waves crash 'gainst the shore,
Felt a need for companion's hand…
To add *her* footprints in the sand…

I was in my early thirties,
My puppy dog was almost two.
Living my dream as an Author,
We could *eat* yesterday again.

With two place mats set at that table,
With puppy dog sat at my feet,
We sat alone at dinner time,
Waiting at the place we'll ne'er meet…

'Sometimes No Time'

Sometimes there is,
Nothing to do,
But relax and unwind,
Where that's just fine!

I wasn't taught that,
When growing up,
It was: *"TIME! TIME! TIME!"*
"THERE IS NO TIME!".

"DO IT PROPERLY!",
"DO IT MY WAY!",
"HOW I LIKE IT!",
"THE ONLY WAY!".

"IF YOU WANT IT,
DONE PROPERLY,
DO IT YOURSELF!".
...Do it yourself then...

Stop berating me,
Stop controlling me,
(Then you'll find there's time,
To relax and unwind...)

"Live your own life.
You do you..."
If only that,
Could ever be true.

'Melancholic Black'

Black bile,
"Black dog",
Black thoughts,
Black mind.

Black mood,
Black hope,
Black clouds,
Black skies.

Black days,
Black nights,
Black dreams,
Black holes.

Black speech,
Black words,
Black sights,
Black Hell.

Black death?
Black plague?
Black breath?
Black lies...

A life where
Everything
Fades to
...Black.

'That Feeling When'

That feeling when eyes meet for the first time.
That feeling when hands find others' hands.
That feeling when our footsteps synchronize.
That feeling when their arm becomes embrace.
That feeling when both heartbeats beat in tune.
That feeling when their body becomes home.
That feeling when their mind inspires your being.
That feeling when each soul becomes entwined.
That feeling when your own heart breaks in two...
That feeling when... you know they're gone for good!

'Miles Of Melancholia'

When I view maps of melancholic mire,
It seems as if I sail through River Styx,
It feels like other passengers are dead,
Where light pulsates and glimmers to then fade...

I know the maps from memory and miles,
Spent lost in black melancholic bile,
'Til I found way back to lands of Living,
But wondered what I brought with me to shore...

O'er each shoulder checking; sensing traps,
As if some shadow-spirit pursued me.
When we return from Realms of the Dead,
How can we truly know we returned *whole?*

'Wrinkles Waste the Sorrow-filled Face'

So tenderly I mourned for you,
As gently forms the morning dew,
Wrinkles waste sorrow-filled face,
To flee from Passion's fleeting embrace.

'The Flow'

What's the rush?
SIMPLY FLOW.
...Flows rush nowhere.
Flows just... go.

They glide and sail,
And move and ride,
Their own currents,
Form unseen tides.

Divinity in human dress,
A Trinity in love bedecked,
Calamity-avoidance power,
Flowing to your final hour.

Live, love, laugh;
Always trust:
The sights that shine,
From *Soul Stardust*.

'Heart Sails'

I went sailing through my heart,
Storms were brewing; I depart.
I went sailing through my mind,
Rain was falling; found me blind.

I went sailing through my soul;
Immortal-self lost in fog.
I went sailing through my body;
Broken bones and unhealed scars.

I went sailing for the shore;
Save my heart, mind, body, soul.
Tattered sails of my heartstrings,
Could not catch the wind, to bring,

Back to bays of brighter days,
Yet vessel ne'er e'er left this room...

'Play Button'

Life feels paused,
Where's the play button?
Youth has vanished,
With all dalliance.

Friendships gone,
Romance ended,
What is left to do,
But breathe?

Hopes forgotten,
Dreams are too,
Memories outcast,
Nightmares looming.

Numb the senses,
Perish thought,
Write words down;
Achieve naught.

Life feels paused,
Where's the play button?
How to find,
A life worth living?

When everything seems,
...So dead and gone.

'To Write That Voice'

To write poetry is a 'nightmare dream',
A soul-task thrust upon you from the Void,
Words sent from subterranean levels,
Erupting forth from a tectonic shift.

Bubbling forth during sleeping hours,
Confusion scatters; terrified by powers,
That grip subconscious faculties by force,
To suddenly speak ancient tongues of verse.

It often arrives when you least suspect,
A distant shadow lingering behind,
Whose silent footsteps are felt yet not heard,
Whose unseen form is felt as It observes...

Determining your readiness with pen...
Destiny is calling but to what end?
Words carry consequence that could condemn.
Fate is arriving; will you let It in?

How many eyes at night-time hours have squinted,
Into blackened Void where poets perish?
How many felt as though they had no choice?
But to record the Voice that wakened them...

'Sing The Saga'

It seems like a hell-bent duty,
To sing the sagas of spent life,
To no-one. Hoping that one day,
They may be heard and valued; later.

Emotions are the currency,
Of writers, authors, poets, scribes.
Where words are forged by Smithy hand.
Hammer striking anvil, sparks galore.

To bring into Creation lore;
Tales to tell... Yet we are long gone.

'Long Gone'

What will I leave behind when I'm long gone?
What will be my long-lasting legacy?
The scars and tattoos of my skin shall rot,
The pulse of my heart will cease and simply stop.

If I died tonight, I'd leave no children,
None to remember name or pass it on.
Only my written words might still remain,
And how many of those have already gone?

It is a strange journey through this One Life,
Our feelings seem so certain like cement,
That there is reason, purpose or intent,
Buried beneath if we should strike the surface...

Perhaps there's not, I never *believed* that.
But this does not mean that it's not the Truth.
How wrong we are whene'er we feel we're right,
How right we are to learn whene'er we're wrong.

Who will sing my song when I can't sing it?
What has been the point of this weary life?
To write down words plucked from lost-vacant hours?
To lose the love that flooded through my heart?

All is changing; everything has altered,
There seems to be no constancy or state,
Wherein peace lasts eternally in bliss,
Perhaps that is what I might inherit?

'Shadow Of Death'

The shadow of death lingers near,
Each waking moment, smile and joy,
Each vacant hour spent in vain,
Each trying time we wished passed by.

Each handshake starting adventure,
Each stormy fist raised in anger,
Each sullen cloud, each spent raindrop,
The shadow of death lingers near.

Even the most fulfilling life,
Must face that shadow when light shines,
Each moment memory in mind,
Can see that shadow lurking by...

We come to terms at night-black shade,
That all our lives shall simply fade.
The laughter, love and life we spent,
Has all but gone to form shadow.

Perhaps that is what dances there,
In our peripheral vision,
The shadow of death lingers near,
When life has been lived *without fear.*

The shadow of death lingers near,
Stepping through, what do we find there?
The shadow of death lingers near,
So jealous of the lives we bear...

'Coffin Chill'

Chills carried on the air of one August midnight,
Brought me to the altar where I will one day lie,
Final sacrifice gifted on my dying breath?
My cold corpse; that ship my soul used to sail life through.

But warmth surrounded it; a Wind that was soul-born,
Carried what is left of me to eternal home.

'The Dig'

Went digging where no human being should go...
Where only sense of dread can e'er be known,
Where souls shall find their torment ever sown,
A place where living breath is never blown.

Went there on vision quest; shamanic trance,
Never can shake the spirits that soon danced,
Around my corporeal light shining,
On which those lost-dead souls were soon dining.

Naïve, young, foolish; such thirst for knowledge,
Shall send so many people over edge,
Has seen me into old man too soon sent,
Where silver hair shall spring straight out the head.

Yet my age is only creaking thirty,
That Dig into Hell has made me dirty!
Not knowing where I went but 'Underworld',
Has seen my vision quest into Doom hurled.

Be careful when you practice scrying arts,
Your soul can splinter into many parts,
Your limited life force can soon depart,
Where lessons learnt can only teach... regret.

<u>Other Written Works by Tadhg Culley</u>

Poetry Books – Available on Amazon
'Undo the Heartbreak' (Anthology of 150 poems)
'Unsung Lyricality' (Anthology of 68 poems)
'Relive the Romance' (Chapbook of 34 poems)
'Red Glows Only Lovers Know' (1 long poem)

Novellas – Available on Amazon
'The Poet And The Prostitute'
'The Holler Screams'
'Gridlock Deadlock'

Short Story Collection – Available on Amazon
'Secrets Buried In The Woods'

Memoir – Available on Amazon
'Paperback Silverback'

Feature Film Screenplays
'Endless Life' (Realist Drama)
'Cold Star' (Gritty Drama)
'Stepping Stones' (Thriller/Horror)
'Tailback' (Thriller)
'Urbex' (Thriller)
'Quarrying Souls' (Supernatural Horror)
'The Long Barrow' (Archaeological Horror)
'Mouth of the Hollow' (Revenge Thriller)
'Our Love Shook The Berlin Wall' (Romance Thriller)
'In Cinemas Now' (Supernatural Horror)

TV Series Screenplays
'Death Duty' (Supernatural Horror)
'Wardens' (Sit Com)

About the Author

Tadhg Culley is a Professional Screenwriter, Published Author and Poet from the UK. He has written ten feature film screenplays, eight TV series scripts, five poetry books, three novellas, three guidebooks, one memoir, one collection of short stories, and many other short-form works, delving into documentary, theatre, animation and games. He is a BAFTA Scholar and graduate of both the National Film & TV School (NFTS) & the University of Creative Arts (UCA).

Printed in Great Britain
by Amazon

65124328R00016